I0798608

10 New Mormon Temples

Counted Cross-stitch Patterns of Temples of The Church of Jesus Christ of Latter-day Saints

Jean D. Crowther

The patterns and instructions in this book were designed and proofread carefully. However, mistakes in printing or individual stitching challenges occasionally occur. We apologize for any inconvenience.

First printing
July, 1997

International Standard Book Number
0-88290-606-2

Horizon Publishers' Catalog and Order Number
2810

Printed and distributed
in the United States of America by

Horizon Publishers

& Distributors, Incorporated

Mailing Address:
P.O. Box 490
Bountiful, Utah 84011-0490

Street Address:
50 South 500 West
Bountiful, Utah 84010

Local Phone: (801) 295-9451
WATS (toll free): 1 (800) 453-0812
FAX: (801) 295-0196

Internet: www.horizonpublishers.com

Table of Contents

Introduction

Members of The Church of Jesus Christ of Latter-day Saints have been counseled to display pictures of the temples in their homes to remind themselves and their families of their eternal goal of exaltation together. These temples have been designed and charted for cross-stitching to help members follow this counsel and to assist them in beautifying their surroundings.

Horizon Publishers and Distributors, Inc. has endeavored, over the years, to provide LDS members with patterns of the new temples as the temple has been announced and the architectural drawings published. This book contains the four newest temples dedicated and six additional temples which are nearing completion at the time of this publication.

It is hoped that these designs will provide stitchers with enjoyment and with lovely pieces of art for themselves and for them to share with their families and friends. May all the recipients draw strength and inspiration for everyday life from having this stitchery in their homes, and may we all be blessed by the guidance, instruction and inspiration received in the sacred temples.

Jean D. Crowther

Acknowledgments

Grateful appreciation is extended to all who helped produce this book:

- Duane S. Crowther, President of Horizon Publishers, who conceived the idea and encouraged the project in numerous ways;
- The technical staff of Horizon Publishers, for their special care in formatting the book;
- Karolyn Kartchner, who stitched the cover model of the Mount Timpanogos Temple; and
- The following companies which provided materials and technical guidance for this book:
  - *Charles Craft* (Laurinburg, NC)
  - *The DMC Corporation* (South Kearny, NJ)
  - *Davis Computer Services, Inc.* (New Orleans, LA)

About the Author

Jean D. Crowther has combined her knowledge of the writer's art and needlework to provide cross-stitch patterns for many LDS temples and other religious symbols and pictures. Tens of thousands of stitched replicas of her designs hang in homes, chapels, seminaries, offices and other edifices worldwide. Her temple patterns are published in *14 New Mormon Temples, 13 New Mormon Temples* and in numerous leaflets and kits. She has also designed the symbols and mottos for the LDS auxiliaries in the books *Especially for Young Women, Especially for Primary,* and *Especially for Women,* as well as portraits of all the LDS prophets in *Prophets of the Restoration.* She has adapted the famous drawings of the well-known Christian artists Frances and Richard Hook in *Jesus and the Children, A Savior is Born,* and *Jesus of Nazareth,* and also crafted an adaptation of daVinci's *The Last Supper.* In addition, she has served as needlecraft editor for Horizon Publishers in creating 28 cross-stitch books from colored pencil graphs submitted by other designers as well as producing three general cross-stitch books of her own: *Murphy Strikes Again, Darling Dinosaurs,* and *Puppies and Pooches.* She is also the author of other books for Latter-day Saints including *What Do I Do Now, Mom?, Growing Up a Mormon, The Joy of Being a Woman, A Mother's Prayer,* and *Book of Mormon Puzzles and Pictures.*

General Instructions

A Helpful Hint for Beginning—After locating the center of the chart and the material, count to the nearest window or vertical shaded area and stitch that first. Continue in the same direction, stitching the vertical windows and shaded areas to the outer right edge of the temple, skipping the main temple color. Return to the center and work the same areas in the other direction. This approach will reduce the number of counting errors because the squares to be counted are fewer. The main colors of the temple will be easy to fill in after the detail work is completed. Study the chart and instructions carefully to identify the different backstitching colors. They are the final stitches to be completed.

Basic Cross-stitch Technique—Form a habit of always stitching in the same direction. This helps your work to have a smooth, uniform appearance. All first diagonals should be in the same direction (see Figure 1). Use a hoop to keep the stitches uniform in tension.

Half Stitches—In some areas, the graph may show a smaller symbol in one corner of a square. To create this partial stitch, work from the corner hole into the center of the square, placing the needle between the threads (See Figure 2). Complete the square with a half-stitch across the other angle or the backstitch outline color where designated. Occasionally there will be a vertical or horizontal half-stitch indicated. These should be stitched with a very shallow v-stitch, crossing from each of the two corner holes to the center of the square (see Figure 3).

Backstitch Outlining—The backstitching should generally be done after all the cross stitching is complete. Anchor the thread and bring the needle up in an appropriate place in the pattern. Place the needle down in the hole behind the initial stitch. Continue working one stitch-length back on top of the fabric and two stitch-lengths forward beneath the fabric to form a solid line (see Figure 4). To create a more gentle angle, sometimes a single backstitch will travel more than two or three squares vertically or horizontally (see Figure 5). Care must be taken with these longer stitches to keep the floss tension even.

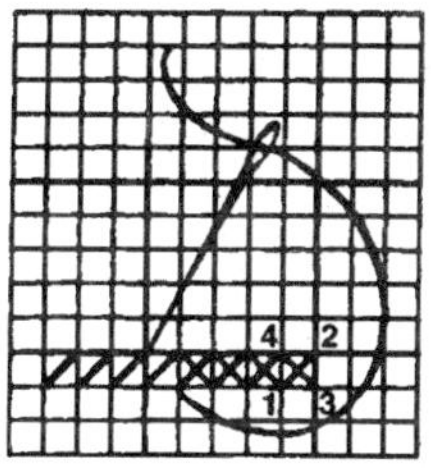

Figure 1
Basic Cross-stitch

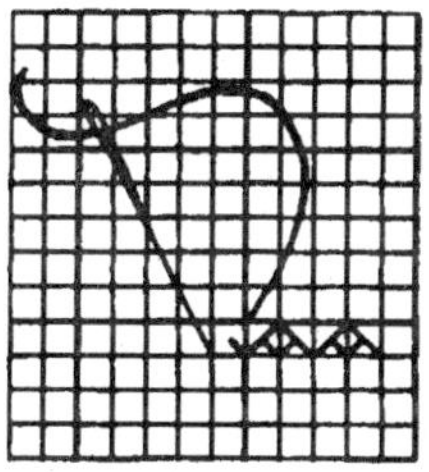
Figure 2
Half Stitch

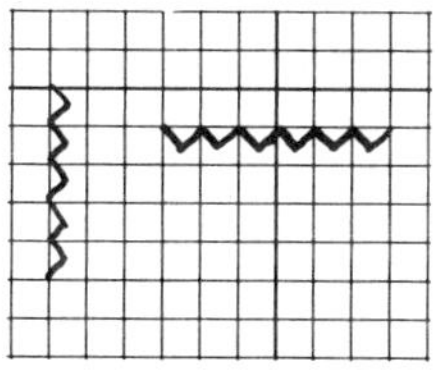
Figure 3
Horizontal or Vertical Half Stitch

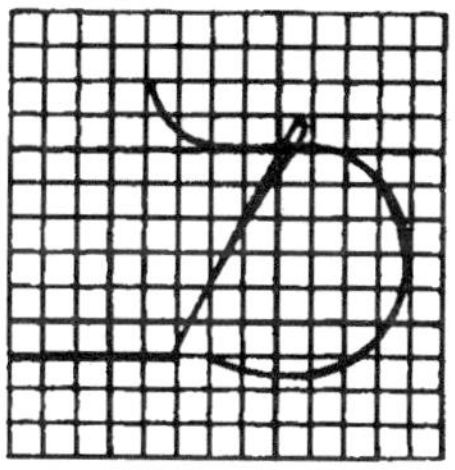
Figure 4
Backstitch Outline

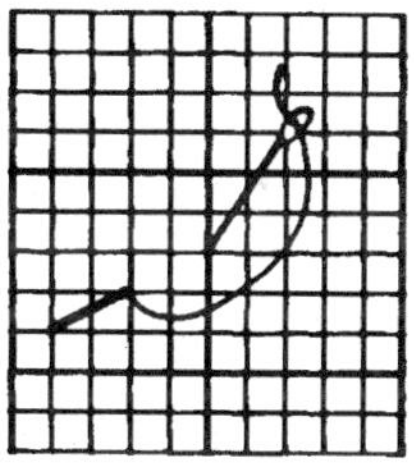
Figure 5
Over-two Backstitch

Slanted Roof Lines and Spires—Most temples in this book have tall spires or roof lines slanted at different angles than is possible to indicate with even the "over-three" stitch. In order to create a relatively accurate angle, a longer line is needed. Study the individual squares of Aida cloth and observe that the material is woven with four threads vertically and crossed with four threads horizontally within the square. (See Figure 6.) This creates five places between threads that the needle can enter the cloth and keep the backstitches evenly placed as the line is created (See Figure 7). Since it is best to use stitches of not more than three squares long, count out the complete length of the backstitch roof or tower line and divide by two or three. This total calculates how many backstitches will be needed for the complete line. Make sure that the thread enters exactly the same exit point of the previous stitch between threads to create a straight line.

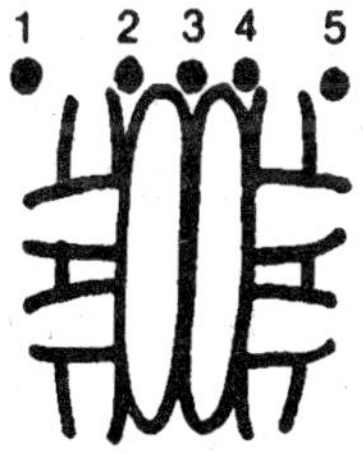

Figure 6
Openings Between Threads

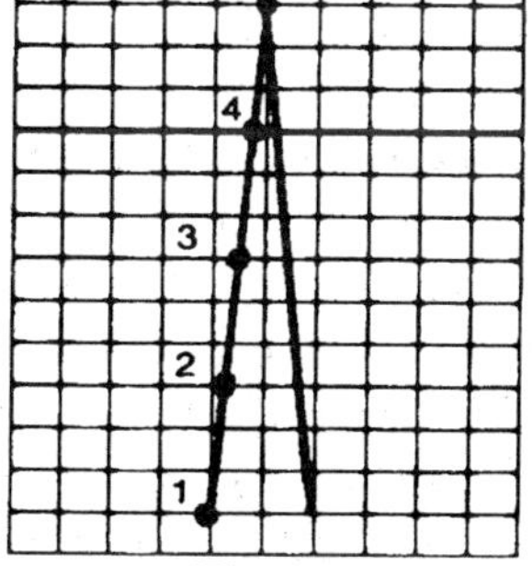

Figure 7
Needle Entry Points

Fill-in Partial Stitches—When working cross stitches to fill in the squares of the areas created by longer backstitch lines, it is necessary to make a different angled stitch. It is easier to leave the partial stitch areas blank until after backstitching. Then carefully create partial stitches, making sure to stay inside the backstitches as your needle enters the material. To fill in next to an "over-two" backstitch, begin at the corner hole of the narrowest square and make a very shallow-angled half stitch. The adjoining square can be filled in with a standard half stitch (See Figure 8). Longer areas will be done in the same manner, increasing the angles as needed (See Figures 9 and 10). When two different colors meet, it is necessary to use the same fill-in techniques for both colors. (See Figure 11).

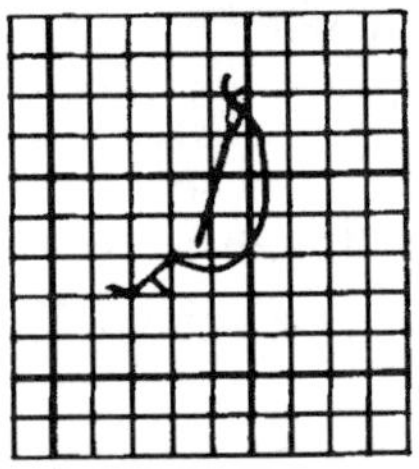

Figure 8
Over-two Fill-in Stitch

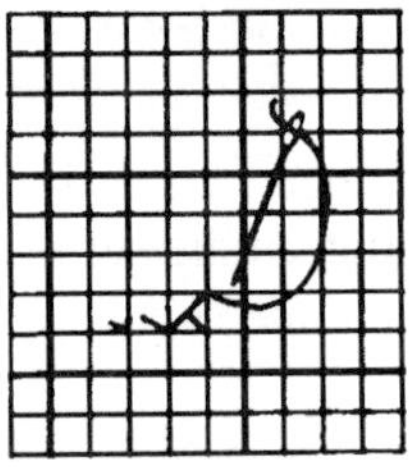

Figure 9
Over-three Fill-in Stitch

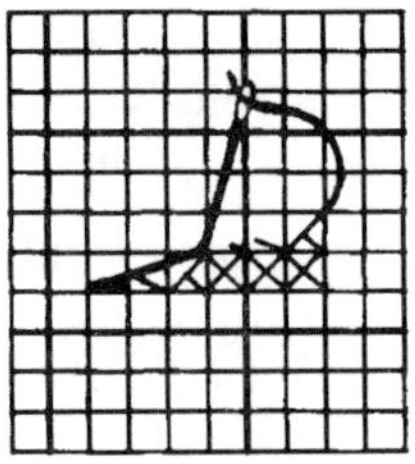

Figure 10
Fill-in Stitches with Over-Three Backstitch

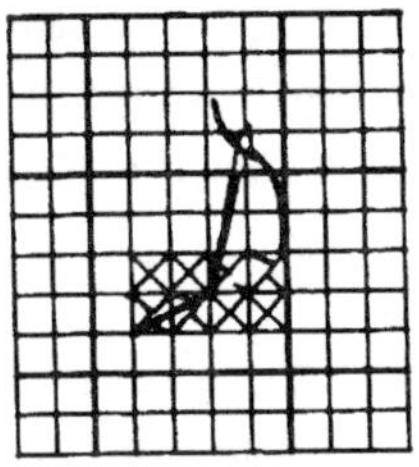

Figure 11
Fill-in Two Colors Meeting with Over-two Backstitch

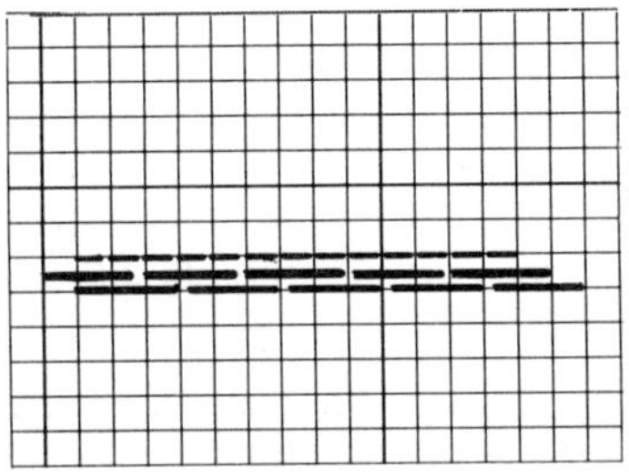

Figure 12
Perle Coton and Floss Ledge Backstitch

Backstitches of Horizontal Ledges—To indicate the architectural detail of horizontal ledges, a technique of using different amounts of floss or *perle coton* has been designed. These horizontal areas are left blank without a cross-stitch color symbol on the charts as the heavier thread will cover the areas. Leave these areas without stitching until the rest of the temple is completed. Then, to create the ledges, first: stitch across the top of the squares with two strands of the basic backstitching color as indicated. Second: stitch across the bottom of the squares with 2-3 strands of white floss, as indicated, stitching over three squares at a time. Lastly: use one strand of #5 *perle coton* down the middle of the squares, stitching over three squares at a time. Make sure that the breaks in the corresponding floss line underneath the perle coton are offset so the ends and beginnings of each stitch are not as obvious. (See Figure 12). A larger tapestry needle will be needed for the *perle coton.*

Backstitches Down the Middle of the Square—Some architectural details are indicated by backstitching down the center of the squares over the background color. Be careful to keep this line straight by finding the center hole (#3 on Figure 6) with every stitch. If these areas are on the edge of the pattern, the fill-in stitch will be made diagonally from the middle of the square to a corner hole. (See Figure 13).

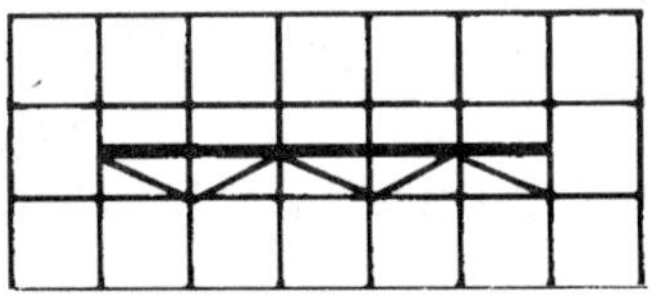

Figure 13
Fill-in Stitches with the Middle of Square Backstitch

Angel Moroni—The angel on top of the temple is indicated by the regular backstitch line surrounded by a dashed line. **Do not stitch the dashed line around the angel on each temple. It is there to separate the gold floss backstitching from the regular backstitch color.** To create a metallic gold appearance, the angel can be worked with gold floss combined with metallic floss or blending filament. The DMC Corporation has developed a metallic floss that is divisible into six strands that is very easy to use. It is suggested that the stitcher begins with two strands of gold floss and one strand of metallic floss in the needle. The ratio of floss to metallic thread can be changed as desired. Note that the angel's head and the ball he stands upon are indicated by a (*). This is worked either in the center of the square or between two squares by first working a normal cross stitch (x) and then a (+) directly on top of the (x), thus creating the round (*). The rest of the angel is finished in a regular backstitch.

Inscription Lines—On some temples, the "House of the Lord" inscription is visible and indicated by backstitch lines. They should be stitched as indicated with two strands of gold floss and, if desired, one strand of metallic floss or blending filament.

Material Needed—The design size (the number of squares covered by the actual design) is given on each chart. The finished size of the temple will be determined by the count of the evenweave fabric used. It can be calculated by dividing the two design size numbers by the number of squares per inch of the material chosen. After determining that measurement, add at least two inches to all four sides of the size to allow adequate material for finishing or framing.

Floss Needed—The general rule is to use one less strand for backstitching than was used for cross stitching. However, more strands may be added to create more distinct lines in the lettering, the window frames and the outline backstitching. The stitcher should experiment in order to achieve the desired effect. When using extra strands of floss, care must be taken to keep the tension even. Suggested amounts are:

Material Count	*Cross-Stitches*	*Backstitching*
11-count Aida	3 strands	2-4 strands
14 or 16-count Aida	2 strands	1-3 strands
18-count Aida	1-2 strands	1-2 strands
Linen worked over two squares	1-2 strands	1-2 strands
22-count Hardanger	1-2 strands	1-2 strands

The color numbers are given for three major brands of floss which are generally available. Listings are given for embroidery floss from The DMC Corporation of Elizabeth, NJ on the individual instruction pages. The corresponding numbers for the Anchor floss, made by Susan Bates of Chester, CT, and Wound Embroidery Floss manufactured by J. & P. Coats of Jacksonville, FL are indicated on page 31. Because of the individual light-reflection characteristics and color-matching differences, the floss from the different companies should not be mixed in a single stitchery design.

Finishing Instructions—Always stitch with clean hands. Even if your completed stitchery doesn't appear soiled, it is best to hand-wash it with mild soap and warm water when finished, just as you would fine lingerie. Rinse the article carefully and blot it with a clean bath towel without wringing, folding, or squeezing the material. Place the wet stitchery, floss-side down, on a dry bath towel, making sure the fabric isn't twisted. Iron until completely dry and the background cloth looks smooth, with the embroidery and background lines straight. In areas where metallic threads are used, a pressing cloth might be needed. Handle the project carefully until it is permanently mounted.

Mount Timpanogos Utah Temple
Instructions

Symbol	DMC #	Color Name	Description
·	762	pale gray	main body of temple
=	415	light gray	light shadows of temple
◆	414	medium gray	medium shadows of temple
—	white	white	tower and trim of temple
I	931	medium slate blue	windows
✱	930	dark slate blue	window shadows
✧	746	cream	tower window
^	3756	baby blue	tower window
+	3823	pale yellow	tower window
<<	954	light green	shrubs and trees
▽	911	emerald green	shrubs and trees
×	white	white	left diagonal fill-in for moonstones*
———	317	dark gray	backstitch outline of temple
-----	white	white	backstitch window frames and ledges
ooooooo	*#5 perle coton*	white	backstitch ledges
•••••••	801	deep brown	backstitch tree trunks
———	3820**	medium gold	Angel Moroni within the dashed lines

Design size: 95 x 85 squares; 95 x 94 with name of temple included.

Special Instructions

Before beginning to stitch this temple, be sure to read the *General Instructions* on pages 5-7 for information on partial stitches, the ledges, and the Angel Moroni.

*Stitch only the left diagonal part of the stitch to fill-in behind the backstitch of the moonstones.

DO NOT STITCH the dashed lines around the Angel Moroni. They are there to indicate that the angel and ball are to be backstitched with gold floss.

**The gold floss can be combined with a metallic floss or blending filament, if desired, to add a gold shine to the project.

The tower windows seem to reflect light differently when viewed from different angles and when the sun is in different positions in the sky. The stained glass effect is designed here. You may choose to work it in #932 for a solid blue or in #597 for the teal blue color sometimes seen.

This temple is located in American Fork, Utah. It was dedicated on October 13, 1996.

Mount Timpanogos Utah Temple Chart

Hong Kong Temple Instructions

Symbol	DMC #	Color Name	Description
·	762	pale gray	main body of temple
\	415	light gray	light shadows of temple
=	318	medium gray	medium shadows of temple
▾	414	dark gray	dark shadows of temple
✧	932	light slate blue	windows
ǀ	930	dark slate blue	window shadows
<<	563	pale green	shrubs and trees
♣	561	forest green	shrubs and trees
/	223	light pink-brown	wall and pillars
○	3721	medium pink-brown	wall and pillars
▼	221	dark pink-brown	wall and pillar shadows
–	3822	bright gold	tower highlights
◆	3820	medium gold	tower
———	413	deep gray	backstitch outline of temple
———	3820*	medium gold	Angel Moroni within the dashed lines
-----	white	white	backstitch window frames

Design size: 72 x 87 squares; 72 x 95 with name of temple included.

Special Instructions

Before beginning to stitch this temple, be sure to read the *General Instructions* on pages 5-7 for information on partial stitches, long backstitch lines, and the Angel Moroni.

DO NOT STITCH the dashed lines around the Angel Moroni. They are there to indicate that the angel and ball are to be backstitched with gold floss.

*The gold floss can be combined with a metallic floss or blending filament, if desired, to add a gold shine to the project.

This temple is located in this building in Hong Kong (China). It was dedicated May 26, 1996.

Hong Kong Temple Chart

St. Louis Missouri Temple Instructions

Symbol	DMC #	Color Name	Description
·	white	white	main body of temple
⁄	415	light gray	light shadows of temple
+	414	medium gray	medium shadows of temple
◂	317	dark gray	dark shadows of temple
–	932	light slate blue	window highlights
∨	931	medium slate blue	windows
❙	930	dark slate blue	window shadows
»	954	light green	shrubs and trees
♣	911	emerald green	shrubs and trees
♥	321	ruby	flowers
———	413	deep gray	backstitch outline of temple
– – – –	414	medium gray	backstitch stonework shadow
-----	white	white	backstitch window frames and ledges
ooooooo	*#5 perle coton*	white	backstitch ledges
———	317	dark gray	backstitch window design*
•••••••	801	deep brown	backstitch tree trunks
------	3820**	medium gold	backstitch inscription
———	3820**	medium gold	Angel Moroni within the dashed lines

Design size: 79 x 87 squares; 79 x 97 with name of temple included.

Special Instructions

Before beginning to stitch this temple, be sure to read the *General Instructions* on pages 5-7 for information on partial stitches, long backstitch lines, the ledges, the inscription and the Angel Moroni.

*The "Star of David" backstitch outline just left of the tower on the graph should be worked in the central top round window just under the inscription. Stitch the window first in #932, medium light blue. Using just one strand of #317, dark gray, work the star with long stitches across the window. Finish the window frame with 2 strands of white floss worked on top of all stitches for the circle and crossed window frames, as indicated.

DO NOT STITCH the dashed lines around the Angel Moroni. They are there to indicate that the angel and ball are to be backstitched with gold floss.

**The gold floss can be combined with a metallic floss or blending filament, if desired, to add a gold shine to the project.

This temple is located in St. Louis, Missouri. It was dedicated on June 1, 1997.

St. Louis Missouri Temple Chart

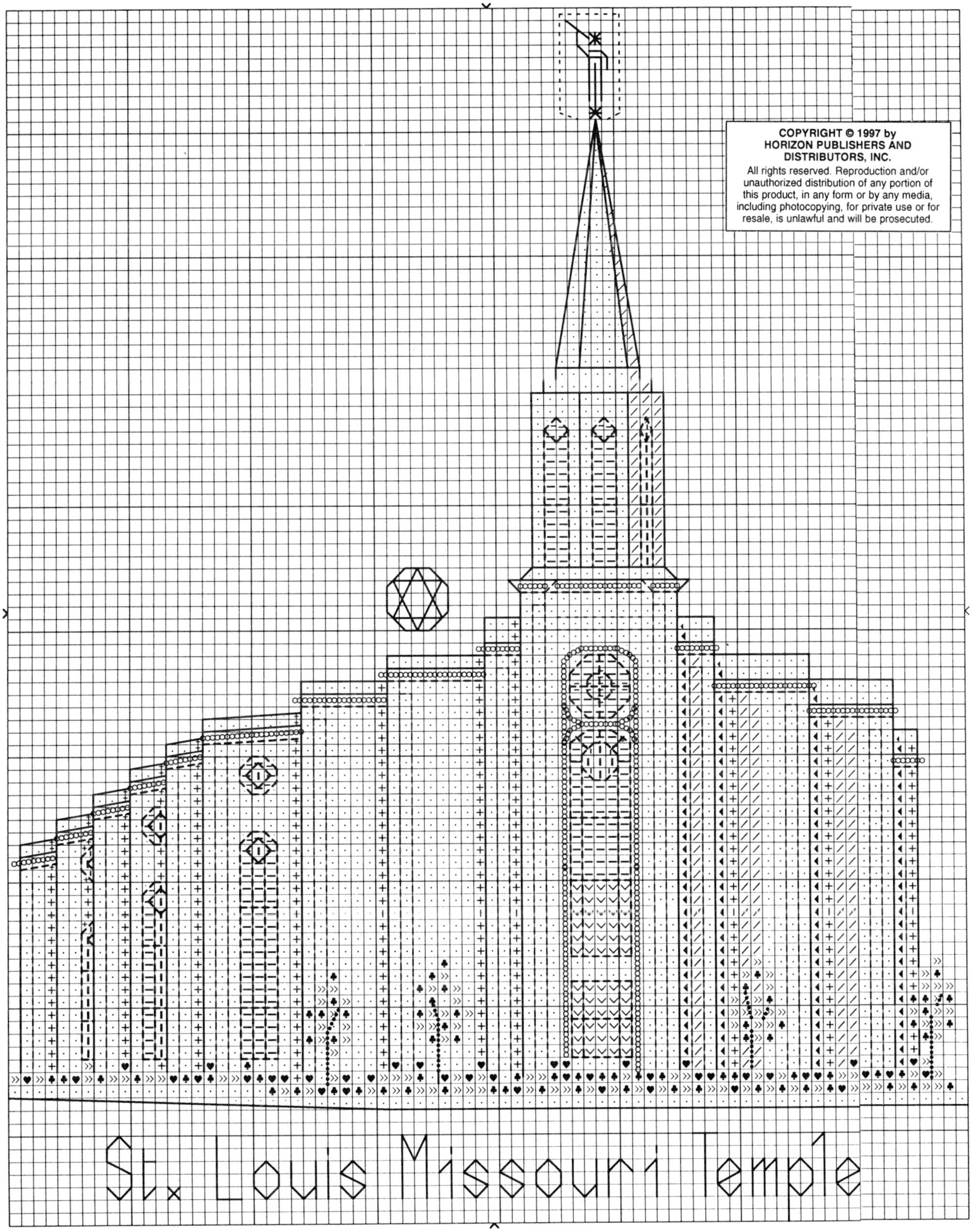

Vernal Utah Temple Instructions

Symbol	DMC #	Color Name	Description
·	758	light brick red	main body of temple
+	356	medium brick red	medium shadows of temple
▼	355	dark brick red	dark shadows of temple
–	3770	light sand	light sandstone window trim
○	3779	medium sand	sandstone wall and fence posts
◣	976	golden brown	front door
»	954	light green	shrubs and trees*
♣	911	emerald green	shrubs and trees*
▽	502	light sage green	roof
▌	501	medium sage green	roof shadows and windows
×	869	weathered copper	tower roofs
/	white	white	roof trim, shadow, and stonework
^	762	pale gray	roof trim shadow
\	307	lemon yellow	stained glass window
✧	334	baby blue	stained glass window
■	340	blue violet	stained glass window
———	3777	deep brick red	backstitch outline of temple
- - - - -	3770	light sand	backstitch sandstone
- - - - - -	500	dark sage green	backstitch roof, towers, and fence
— — — —	white	white	backstitch window frames
•••••••	3820**	medium gold	backstitch inscription and cornerstone
———	3820**	medium gold	Angel Moroni within the dashed lines

Design size: 107 x 61 squares; 107 x 71 with name of temple included.

Special Instructions

Before beginning to stitch this temple, be sure to read the *General Instructions* on pages 5-7 for information on partial stitches, speciality stitches, long backstitch lines, and the Angel Moroni.

*The landscaping was not in place when this temple was designed and the book published. The bushes and small trees were added to the areas where planting boxes were left during the construction. Local stitchers may wish to change the pattern to match these areas as the bushes and small trees are placed.

DO NOT STITCH the dashed lines around the Angel Moroni. They are there to indicate that the angel and ball are to be backstitched with gold floss.

**The gold floss can be combined with a metallic floss or blending filament, if desired, to add a gold shine to the project.

This temple is under construction in Vernal, Utah as this book is printed. The ground was broken May 13, 1995. The dedication date has been announced as November 2, 1997.

Vernal Utah Temple Chart

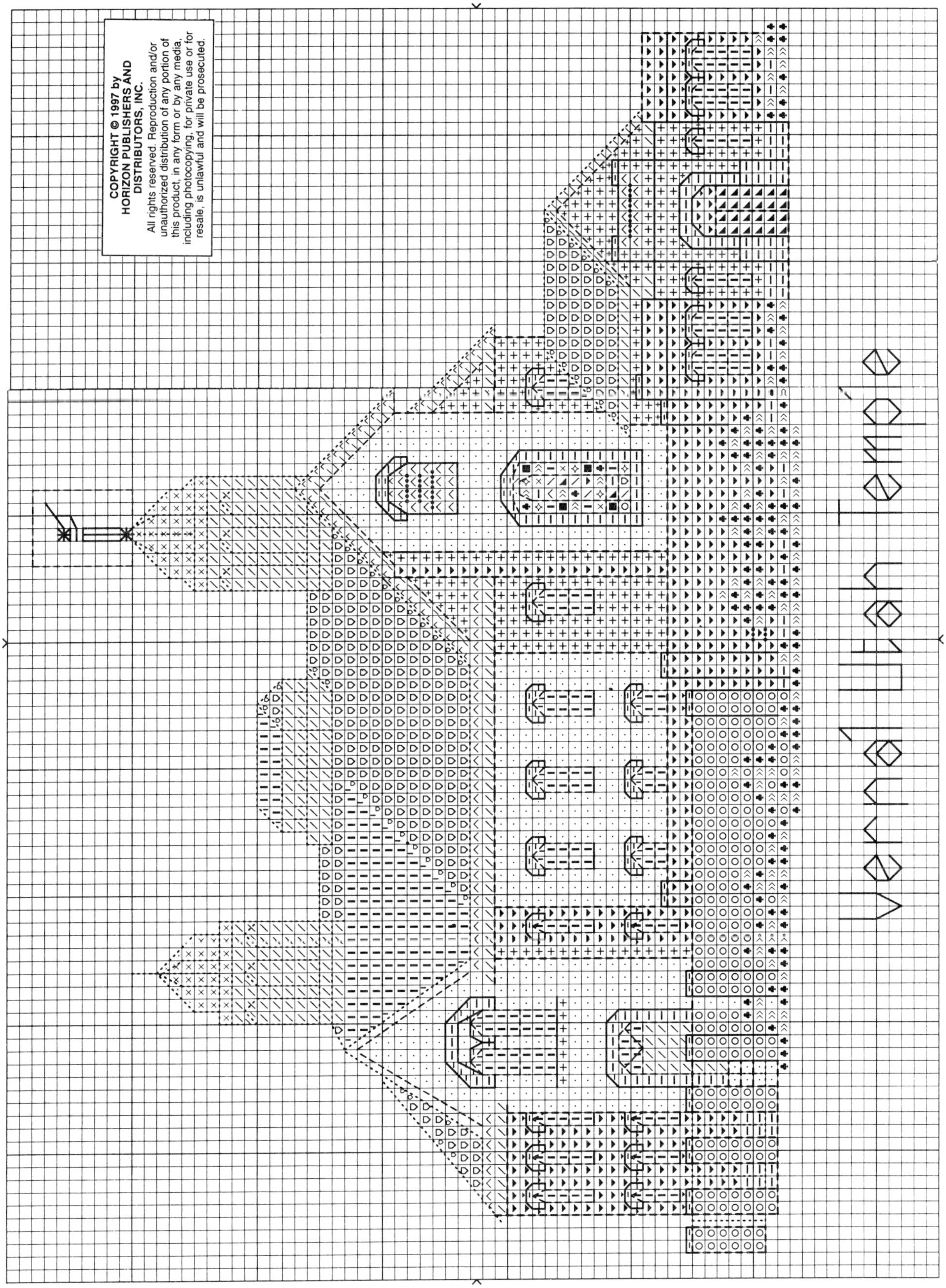

Preston England Temple Instructions

Symbol	DMC #	Color Name	Description
·	762	pale gray	main body of temple
\	415	light gray	light shadows of temple
○	318	medium gray	medium shadows of temple
▸	414	dark gray	dark shadows of temple
∨	334	alice blue	windows
▮	312	dark alice blue	window shadows
■	780	deepest gold	doors of temple
»	563	pale green	shrubs and trees
♣	561	forest green	shrubs and trees
———	413	deep gray	backstitch outline of temple
– – – –	414	medium gray	backstitch stone shadow
- - - - -	white	white	backstitch window frames
•••••••	801	deep brown	backstitch tree trunks
------	3820*	medium gold	backstitch inscription
———	3820*	medium gold	Angel Moroni within the dashed lines

Design size: 63 x 92 squares; 63 x 102 with name of temple included.

Special Instructions

Before beginning to stitch this temple, be sure to read the *General Instructions* on pages 5-7 for information on partial stitches, speciality stitches, long backstitch lines, the tower, the inscription, and the Angel Moroni.

DO NOT STITCH the dashed lines around the Angel Moroni. They are there to indicate that the angel and ball are to be backstitched with gold floss.

*The gold floss can be combined with a metallic floss or blending filament, if desired, to add a gold shine to the project.

This temple is under construction in Preston, England as this book is printed. The ground was broken on June 12, 1994.

Preston England Temple Chart

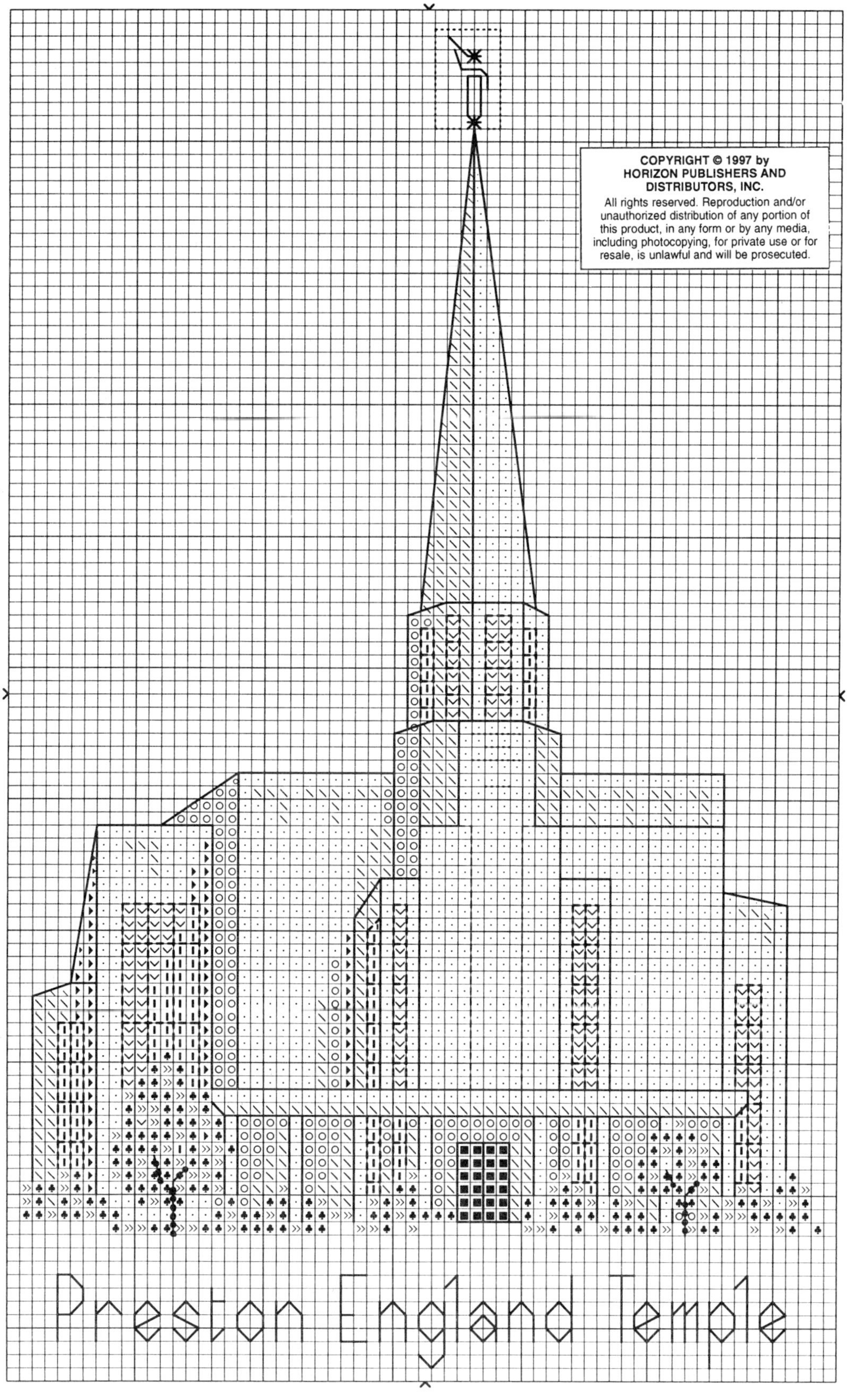

Madrid Spain Temple Instructions

Symbol	DMC #	Color Name	Description
·	white	white	main body of temple
\	415	light gray	light shadows of temple
×	414	medium gray	medium shadows of temple
▽	340	periwinkle blue	windows
▶	333	dark periwinkle	window shadows and door
◒	434	dark brown	door frame
+	902	burgundy	tall windows
I	367	dark grass green	shrubs and trees
^	437	light brown	brick planting boxes
◀	435	medium brown	brick planting boxes shadows
———	413	deep gray	backstitch outline of temple
- - - - -	902	burgundy	backstitch narrow tall windows
———	3820*	medium gold	Angel Moroni within the dashed lines
———	*#5 perle coton*	white	backstitch diagonal lattice work**

Design size: 109 x 83 squares; 109 x 93 with name of temple included.

Special Instructions

Before beginning to stitch this temple, be sure to read the *General Instructions* on pages 5-7 for information on partial stitches, long backstitch lines, and the Angel Moroni.

DO NOT STITCH the dashed lines around the Angel Moroni. They are there to indicate that the angel and ball are to be backstitched with gold floss.

*The gold floss can be combined with a metallic floss or blending filament, if desired, to add a gold shine to the project.

There are 12 open areas in the tower. They are left unstitched.

**The beautiful stone lattice work at the front of the temple is indicated on the chart by diagonal lines between the pillars. The diagonal lines should be stitched with one strand of #5 white *perle coton* working over 2-3 squares at a time, as indicated. After the diagonal lines are finished, the entire rectangle should be backstitched with #413, deep gray.

This temple is under construction in Madrid, Spain as this book is printed. The ground was broken on June 11, 1996.

Madrid Spain Temple Chart

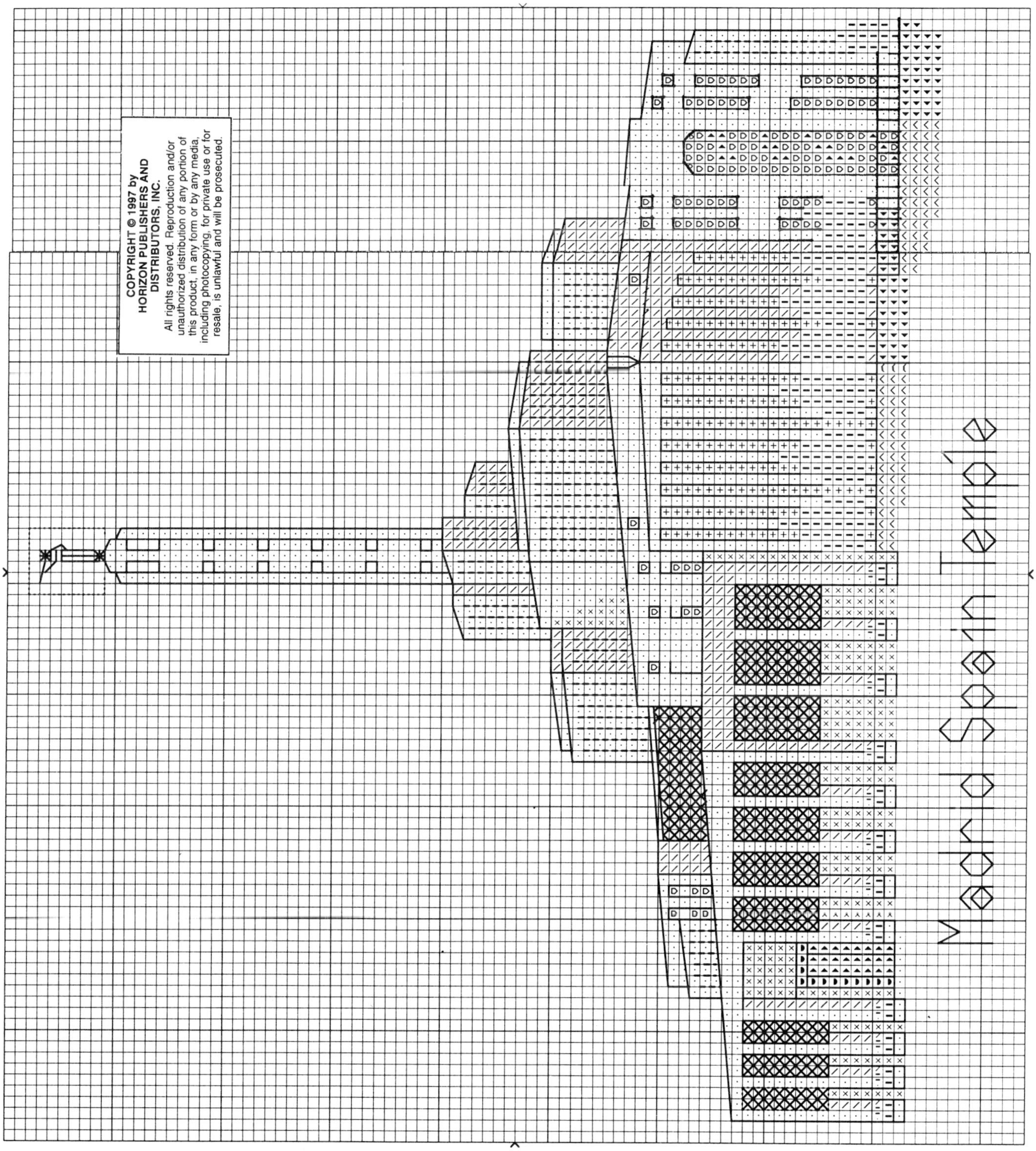

Bogota Columbia Temple Instructions

Symbol	DMC #	Color Name	Description
·	white	white	main body of temple
╲	762	pale gray	light shadows of temple
^	318	medium gray	medium shadows of temple
+	333	dark periwinkle	windows and flowers
=	340	periwinkle blue	window shadows and flowers
▸	320	medium grass green	shrubs and trees
✧	780	deepest gold	door of temple
———	413	deep gray	backstitch outline of temple
-----	white	white	backstitch window frames and ledges
ooooooo	#5 *perle coton*	white	backstitch ledges
•••••••	801	deep brown	backstitch tree trunks
– – – –	3820*	medium gold	backstitch stair railing
———	3820*	medium gold	Angel Moroni within the dashed lines

Design size: 84 x 64 squares; 84 x 74 with name of temple included.

Special Instructions

Before beginning to stitch this temple, be sure to read the *General Instructions* on pages 5-7 for information on partial stitches, long backstitch lines, ledges, and the Angel Moroni.

DO NOT STITCH the dashed lines around the Angel Moroni. They are there to indicate that the angel and ball are to be backstitched with gold floss.

*The gold floss can be combined with a metallic floss or blending filament, if desired, to add a gold shine to the project.

This temple is under construction in Bogota, Columbia as this book is printed. The ground was broken on June 26, 1993.

Bogota Columbia Temple Chart

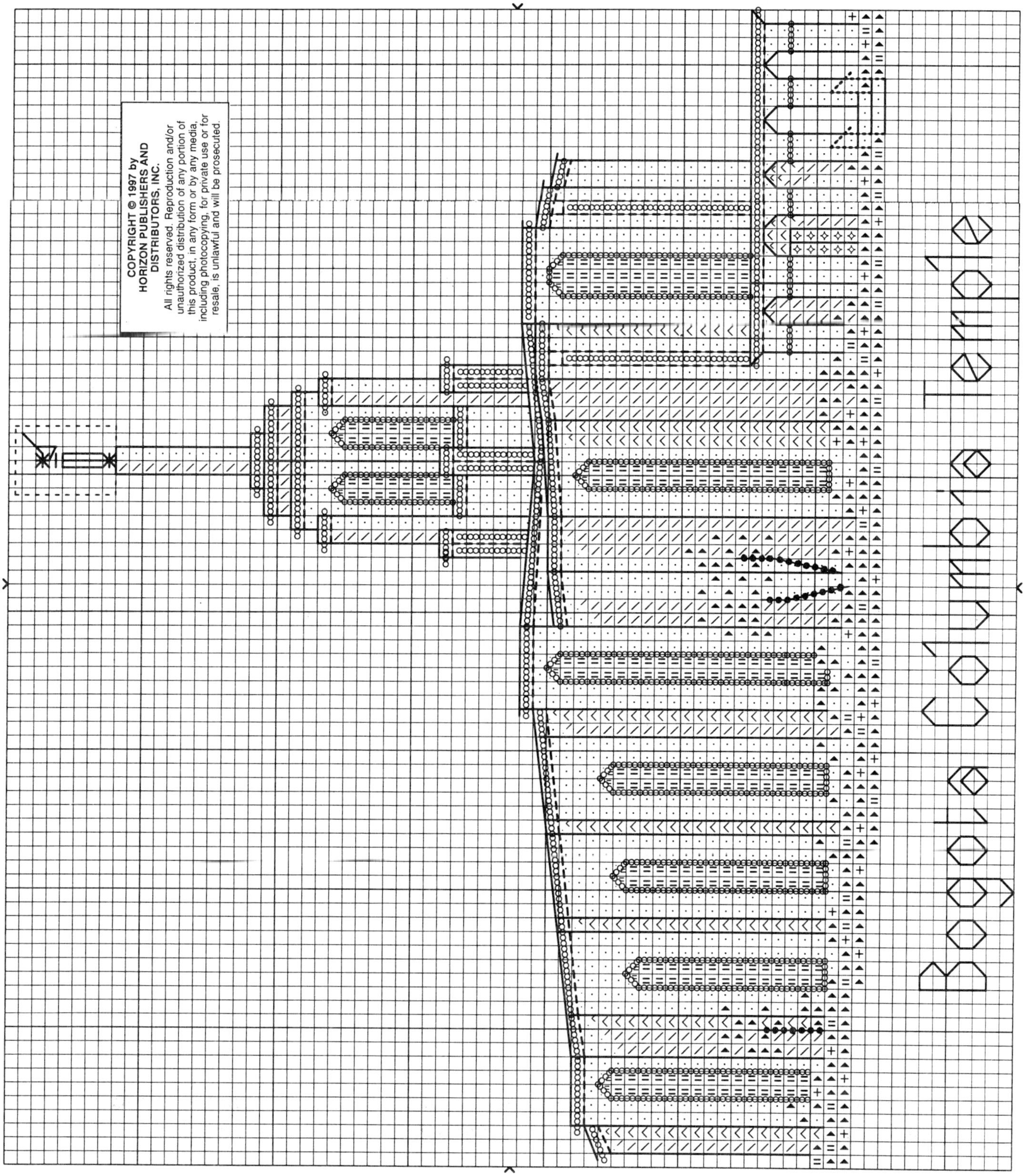

Santo Domingo Dominican Republic Temple Instructions

Symbol	DMC #	Color Name	Description
·	712	ivory	main body of temple
\	822	light beige	light shadows of temple
+	3023	light gray brown	medium shadows of temple
×	340	periwinkle blue	windows
»	563	pale green	shrubs
♣	561	forest green	trees and shrubs
♥	894	coral	flowers
•••••••	801	deep brown	backstitch tree trunks
-----	712	ivory	backstitch window frames and ledges
———	3787	dark gray-brown	backstitch outline of temple
ooooooo	746 *#5 perle coton*	cream	backstitch ledges and stonework
– – – –	3820*	medium gold	backstitch inscription
———	3820*	medium gold	Angel Moroni within the dashed lines

Design size: 81 x 80 squares; 81 x 95 with name of temple included.

Special Instructions

Before beginning to stitch this temple, be sure to read the *General Instructions* on pages 5-7 for information on partial stitches, ledges, long backstitch lines, the inscription and the Angel Moroni.

DO NOT STITCH the dashed lines around the Angel Moroni. They are there to indicate that the angel and ball are to be backstitched with gold floss.

*The gold floss can be combined with a metallic floss or blending filament, if desired, to add a gold shine to the project.

This temple is under construction in Santo Domingo, Dominican Republic as this book is printed. The ground was broken on August 8, 1996.

Santo Domingo Dominican Republic Temple Chart

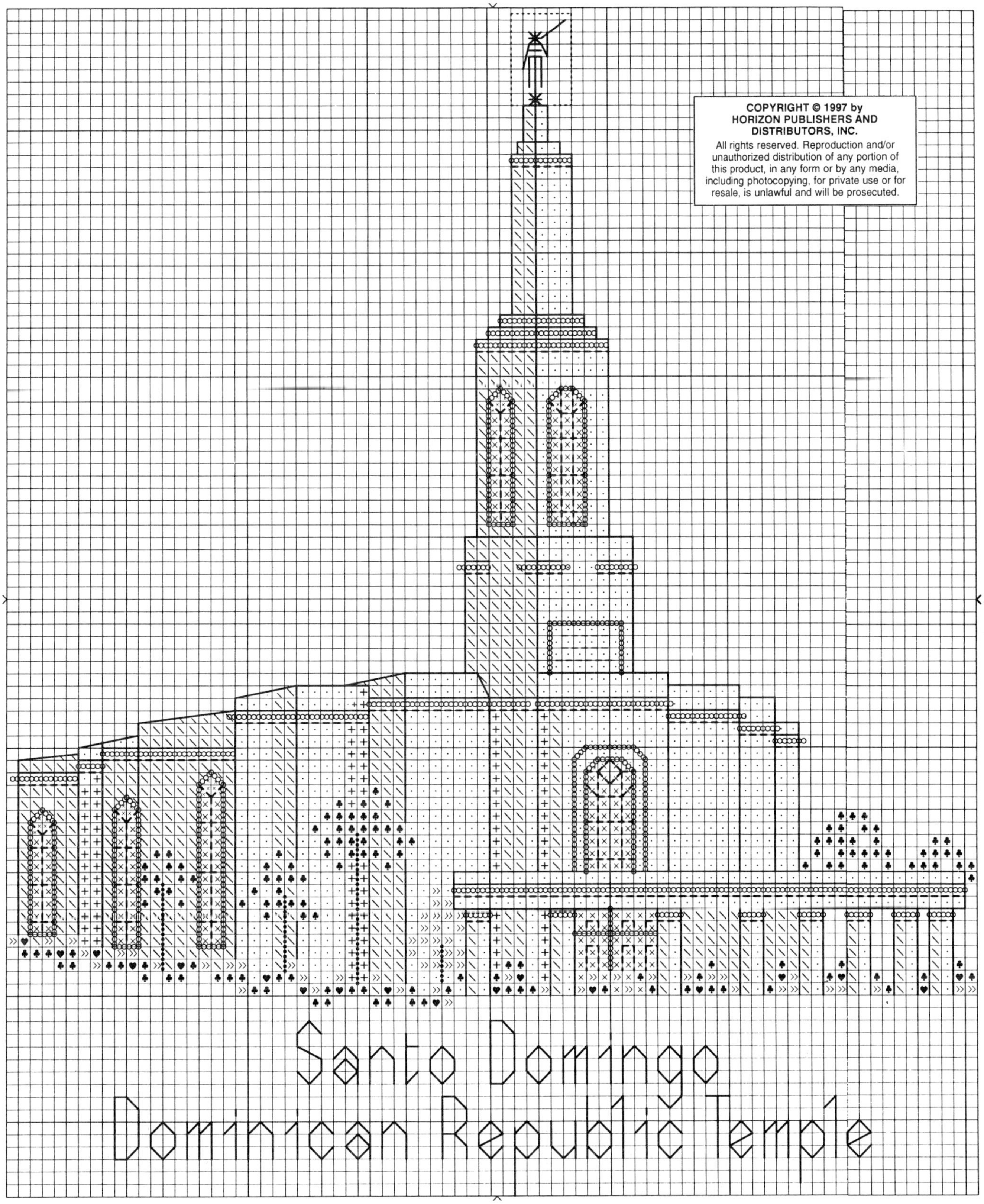

Guayaquil Ecuador Temple Instructions

Symbol	DMC #	Color Name	Description
·	white	white	main body of temple
＼	415	light gray	light shadows of temple
^	318	medium gray	medium shadows of temple
+	414	dark medium gray	dark shadows of temple
‖	312	dark alice blue	windows
○	334	alice blue	window highlights
♣	369	light grass green	shrubs and trees
«	367	dark grass green	shrubs and trees
♥	894	coral	flowers
———	317	deep gray	backstitch outline of temple
- - - -	318	dark medium gray	backstitch stone shadow
-----	white	white	backstitch window frames, ledges
ooooooo	#5 *perle coton*	white	backstitch ledges
•••••••	801	deep brown	backstitch tree trunks
———	3820*	medium gold	Angel Moroni within the dashed lines

Design size: 76 x 70 squares; 76 x 79 with name of temple included.

Special Instructions

Before beginning to stitch this temple, be sure to read the *General Instructions* on pages 5-7 for information on partial stitches, long backstitch lines, the ledges, long backstitches, the tower, and the Angel Moroni.

DO NOT STITCH the dashed lines around the Angel Moroni. They are there to indicate that the angel and ball are to be backstitched with gold floss.

*The gold floss can be combined with a metallic floss or blending filament, if desired, to add a gold shine to the project.

This temple is under construction in Guayaquil, Ecuador as this book is printed. It was announced in 1982 but construction was delayed. The ground was broken on August 10, 1996.

Guayaquil Ecuador Temple Chart

Bountiful Utah Temple Instructions

Symbol	DMC #	Color Name	Description
·	white	white	main body of temple
⁄	415	light gray	light shadows of temple
∧	414	medium gray	medium shadows of temple
+	931	medium slate blue	tall windows
–	3752	pale slate blue	tall window highlights
✱	3820/white*	gold/white	decorative windows
\	3820/414*	gold/medium gray	decorative windows
■	976	golden brown	door
«	954	light green	shrubs and trees
♣	911	emerald green	shrubs and trees
○	894	coral	flowers
♥	321	ruby	flowers
×	white	white	left diagonal fill-in for moonstones**
———	317	dark gray	backstitch outline of temple
-----	white	white	backstitch window frames
ooooooo	*#5 perle coton*	white	backstitch ledges
•••••••	801	deep brown	backstitch tree trunks
+++++++	561	forest green	backstitch evergreen tree
– – – –	3820***	gold	backstitch inscription and cornerstone
———	3820***	gold	Angel Moroni within the dashed lines

Design size: 100 x 91 squares; 100 x 99 with name of temple included.

Special Instructions

Before beginning to stitch this temple, be sure to read the *General Instructions* on pages 5-7 for information on partial stitches, long backstitch lines, the ledges, the tower, and the Angel Moroni.

*Use one strand of each color in the needle together to create the decorative effect.

**Stitch only the left diagonal part of the stitch to fill-in behind the backstitch of the moonstones.

DO NOT STITCH the dashed lines around the Angel Moroni. They are there to indicate that the angel and ball are to be backstitched with gold floss.

***The gold floss can be combined with a metallic floss or blending filament, if desired, to add a gold shine to the project.

The two sunstones on each side of the tower should both be stitched with the 15-spoked backstitch design charted on the left of the tower. Use 1 strand of #317 and make long stitches from the outside end of each line toward the center, making sure to keep the tension even and the stitches entering the same exact center hole.

This temple is located in Bountiful, Utah. It was dedicated on January 8, 1995.

Bountiful Utah Temple Chart

Borders Instructions

These six borders are charted to be stitched around the temples.They are designed to be done in two colors which should be chosen by the stitcher.

The #1 ***Time and Eternity*** border is designed to be used for any of the temples in this book. It measures a total of 138 x 179 squares and can be used either vertically or horizontally. The inside open space measures 114 x 147 so there is room inside the border for the temple and additional personalization areas.

The #2 to #6 borders will need to be calculated to fit the temple stitched. Examine the chosen border carefully to see that it is made up of corner motifs and repeating side motifs. Add ten squares to all four sides of the complete temple dimensions to know the inside measurements of the border needed.

With a pencil, draw the outline of the design size of two of the corner motifs at the corner places of the inside measurements of the border needed on graph paper. Calculate how many squares there are between them. Divide the horizontal count of a side motif design size into that distance. It then might be necessary to move the corners motifs in or out a few squares to make room for a complete side motif. Repeat this procedure with a third corner.

Be sure to not crowd the temple inside the border. Allow about 6-10 squares, or at least one-half inch, between the outside stitch area of the temple and the border. It should not be necessary to graph out a complete border once the two sides and three corners are worked out.

Border name	**Corner motif design size**	**Side motif design size**
#2 *Large Hearts*	10 x 10 squares	9 x 10 squares (connected with one shared linking square)
#3 *Small Hearts*	5 x 5 squares	5 x 5 squares (connected with one unshared linking square)
#4 *Geometric*	7 x 7 squares	2 x 7 squares
#5 *Interlocking Rings*	13 x 13 squares (three total rings)	9 x 9 squares (one single ring)
#6 *Solid Outside*	5 x 5 squares	2 x 5 squares

Borders Charts

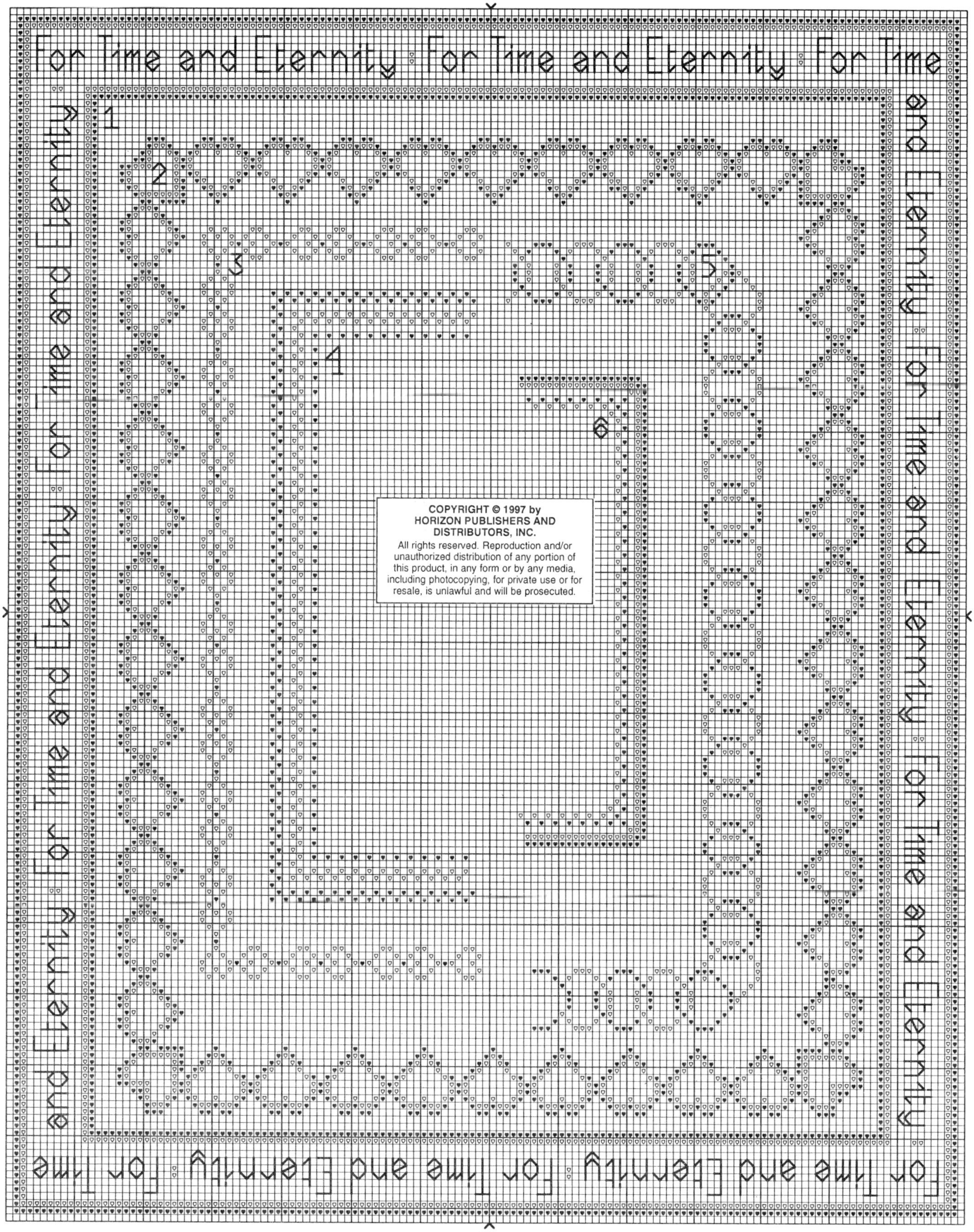

Alphabet Instructions and Chart

The small alphabet is used for the names of the temples charted in this book.It also can be used for additional personalization of the projects.The large alphabet can be used as is, or color can be added in the empty squares. In general, allow a single square between letters and three squares between words. Center each line, using the centering arrow of the temple as the beginning reference. Be sure to add the extra line count into the total design-size calculations of the temple before beginning to stitch.

Floss Needed and Conversion Chart

The three major floss companies manufacture separate color pallets. Although there is some effort to match basic colors, the floss finishes and color shadings are different for each company. If floss from different companies is mixed in one project, those areas will stand out. This chart will aid the stitcher in selecting her choice of floss. Occasionally there are not enough shades in a single color family, so a possible substitute is indicated in parentheses. Personal tastes might differ. Stitchers should substitute carefully, surveying what the change will mean by spreading the floss out on the cloth to see what the complete effect will be.

Color name	DMC	Anchor	J.P.Coats	Mt. Timp	Hong Kong	St.Louis	Preston	Vernal	Madrid	Bogota	Dom.Rep.	Ecuador	Bountiful	Moroni
dark pink-brown	221	897	2339		X									
light pink-brown	223	893	2337		X									
lemon yellow	307	301	2288					X						
dark alice blue	312	147	7979				X					X		
dark gray	317	401	8514	X		X						X	X	
dark-medium gray	318	399	8511		X		X			X		X		
medium grass green	320	216	6017							X				
ruby	321	19	3000			X							X	
dark periwinkle	333	119	7150						X	X				
alice blue	334	145	7977				X	X				X		
periwinkle blue	340	118	7110					X	X	X	X			
dark brick red	355	5968	2339					X						
medium brick red	356	5975	2338					X						
dark grass green	367	217	6018						X			X		
light grass green	360	214	0010									X		
deep gray	413	(401)	8999	X	X	X	X		X	X				
medium gray	414	400	8512	X	X	X	X		X			X	X	
light gray	415	398	8398	X	X	X	X		X			X	X	
dark brown	434	370	5000						X					
medium brown	435	365	5371						X					
light brown	437	362	5942						X					
dark sage green	500	879	6880					X						
medium sage green	501	878	6878					X						
light sage green	502	876	6876					X						
forest green	561	212	6212		X		X				X		X	
pale green	563	208	6210		X		X				X			
light gold	676	891	5363											X
pale gold	677	292	2305											X
ivory	712	387	5387								X			
cream	746	926	1002	X										
light brick red	758	9575	2337					X						
pale gray	762	397	8510	X	X		X	X		X				
deepest gold	780	310	5309				X			X				X
dark gold	782	309	5308											X
medium gold	783	308	5307											X
deep brown	801	359	5475	X		X	X			X	X	X	X	
light beige	822	926	5830								X			
weathered copper	869	375	944					X						
coral	894	26	3126								X	X	X	
burgundy	902	20	3021						X					
emerald green	911	230	6031	X		X		X					X	
dark slate blue	930	978	7052	X	X	X								
medium slate blue	931	977	7051	X		X							X	
light slate blue	932	976	7050		X	X								
light green	954	204	6020	X		X		X					X	
golden brown	976	308	2308					X					X	
light gray-brown	3023	390	5831								X			
medium pink-brown	3721	896	2338		X									
pale slate blue	3752	975	7876										X	
baby blue	3756	128	7976	X										
light sand	3770	778	3146					X						
deep brick red	3777	(5968)	(2339)					X						
medium sand	3779	882	3868					X						
dark gray-brown	3787	393	5393								X			
medium gold	3820	307	2307	X	X	X	X	X	X	X	X	X	X	
medium gold	3821	306	(2305)											X
bright gold	3822	305	5363		X									
pale yellow	3823	386	2292	X										
white	white	1	1001	X	X	X	X	X	X	X		X	X	
white perle coton	white	1		X		X			X	X		X	X	
cream perle coton	746	926									X			

Angel Moroni Instructions

Symbol	DMC #	Color Name	Description
·	677	pale gold	highlights
╲	676	light gold	light areas
×	3821	gold	main color
♥	783	medium gold	dark shadows
■	782	dark gold	deep shadows
———	780	deepest gold	backstitch outline

Design size: 37 x 96 squares.

Special Instructions

Before beginning to stitch this design, please be sure to read the *General Instructions* on pages 5-7 for information on partial stitches and long backstitch lines.

A gold blending filament or metallic floss can be added to some colors, such as the main color, to give a sparkle to the stitching. It will be too much to add metallic thread to all colors.

The Angel Moroni statue is placed on a tower of most of the temples of the Church. It signifies that he is the angel spoken of in Revelation 14:6-7, D & C 27:5 and D & C 128:20 as the one bringing the everlasting gospel to the world.

The statues on the various temples are not the same, having been designed by different sculptors. They are all similar in that the angel is standing on top of a gold ball, facing in an easterly direction, and holding the trumpet in his outstretched right hand.

This design is adapted from the Angel Moroni on top of the Salt Lake Temple.

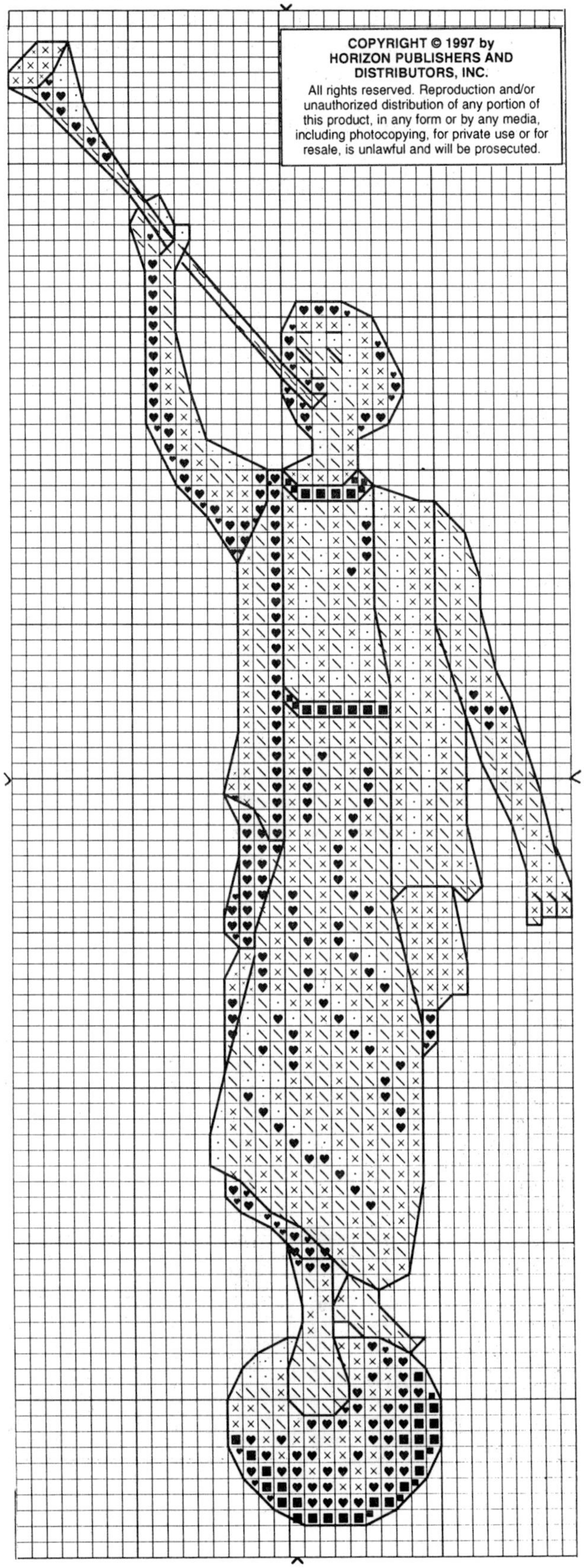